LEARNING THE BUSINESS

ONE STORY AT A TIME

Simple Steps To Super Success

STUDY. DO. TEACH.

LEARNING
THE
BUSINESS

ONE STORY AT A TIME

MICHAEL S. CLOUSE

Nexera™ LLC Publishers *Lynnwood, Washington U.S.A.*

LEARNING THE BUSINESS
ONE STORY AT A TIME

Published by Nexera™ LLC

© 2004 by Michael S. Clouse

International Standard Book Number: 0-9635949-5-8

Nexera™ LLC
18423 – 12th Avenue West
Lynnwood, WA 98037-4900 U.S.A.

ltb@nexera.com
www.nexera.com/ltb

U.S.A. 1 888 639 3722 International +1 425 774 4264

10 9 8 7 6 5 4 3 2

ADVANCED PRAISE

FOR

LEARNING THE BUSINESS
ONE STORY AT A TIME

"Michael is one of the best speakers and trainers I've ever seen... Now he's put 24 of his best trainings—from how to build a better business to how to design a better life—into a wonderful book. *Learning The Business One Story At A Time* is destined to become a Network Marketing classic, and should be read by everyone on your team."

Rita Davenport CSP, CPAE
President, Arbonne International

"Michael's genius (and I rarely use that word) for this industry is captured throughout this incredible book. *Learning The Business One Story At A Time* is a truth filled, fun to read, and dead on target insider look at how to achieve success in Network Marketing. It is obvious that Michael has lived what he has written, and we all are better off because of it... Brilliant."

Doug Firebaugh, CEO
PassionFire International

"*Learning The Business One Story At A Time* will teach you how to build a Network Marketing business... If you want to find more prospects, develop more leaders, and earn more money, read this most excellent book!"

Orjan Saele
Seven Presidential Distributor
The #1 income earner in Scandinavia

"*Learning The Business One Story At A Time* affirms why you are at the top of my list of favorite trainers/mentors in our industry. You've hit another home run!"

Donna Johnson
Executive National Vice President
Arbonne International

"*Learning The Business One Story At A Time* is a must-read treasure-trove of information containing valuable insight for new distributors and veteran Network Marketers alike. Michael's common sense approach to Network Marketing comes through loud and clear!"

Tom Paredes
International Speaker/Trainer

"Since 1985 I've acquired hundreds of books, audios, and videos on our industry. Michael's new book, *Learning The Business One Story At A Time* is one of the best. I would consider it a must-read for both new and experienced Network Marketers, although must-study would be more accurate. Read it, think about it, apply it... and then, read it again."

Gary Wells
Professional Network Marketer

"*Learning The Business One Story At A Time* is a fabulous book brimming over with the quality of MLM wisdom that can only come from actually building an empire. It is simple, engagingly written, and dead on accurate. I will offer it to all my leaders."

Richard Bliss Brooke
Owner, Oxyfresh.com
MLM Hall of Fame Member
Author of Mach 2 with Your Hair on Fire

"I've been a student of Network Marketing since 1975, and have read almost every book written on the subject. *Learning The Business One Story At A Time* is by far the best presentation of what it really takes to develop a viable, life long, successful business... Anyone who has a desire to turn their dreams into reality needs to have this book in their library, apply the principles outlined, and refer to it often."

Dennis L. Williams
Nikken Royal Ambassador

"*Learning The Business One Story At A Time* is one of the most concise and well drafted documents of what Network Marketing is, and is not, I have ever read. This collection of truths along with the basics of how to succeed in Network Marketing is a must-read for every person in this business. You have found a way to capture the essence of what I have learned, believed, and taught for the past 23 years. Congratulations!"

Scott W. Olsen
V.P. of Field Development
Monarch Health Sciences

"Michael has unleashed his teaching power in the book you are about to read. The philosophies and wisdom contained in *Learning The Business One Story At A Time* will not only give you and your business new life, they are more valuable than silver and gold."

Frank AuCoin
South Carolina Businessman of the Year

TABLE OF CONTENTS

DEDICATION

Learning The Business One Story At A Time is respectfully dedicated to one of the greatest storytellers who ever lived, Og Mandino.

I first heard Og Mandino's name sometime in the mid 1980's in the corner office of Chuck Crocker, a second level manager working the credit and collections side of AT&T's GBS division. Although I don't recall the day, year, or even the exact conversation, I do remember Chuck letting me borrow his personal copy of *The Greatest Salesman in the World* by Og Mandino.

Years later I personally met Og Mandino on two different occasions. Our first encounter was on Tuesday, May 18, 1993 just before his book signing for *The Twelfth Angel* at Brentano's Bookstore in Seattle, Washington. I'm quite certain of the date and location, because our conversation meant so much to me that to this day I still have the yellow photocopied flyer providing those details tucked neatly inside the dust jacket of my personally autographed copy of that book.

The next time our lives came together was at an event in Dallas, Texas. Og was there to share his stories with a few thousand enthusiastic entrepreneurs, and I was fortunate enough to be a part of his audience. And because he was a gracious man, after Og had finished speaking, he signed books for nearly three hours. I was the last person in line—the last person to have my picture taken with Og Mandino.

Although Og Mandino is no longer with us, the lives he touched and his wonderful stories live on....

May 2004

INTRODUCTION

A wise man once defined life as, "A collection of experiences and their intensity." How true. And as I patiently ponder the past 18+ years I've been involved—one way or another—in this industry, it's quite clear I too have indeed assembled my own unique assortment of people, places, and parables—or stories—along the way...

However, what you may find considerably more captivating is the *connection*—the connection between the people you meet, the places you visit, and the stories that you too will pick up on your journey. Let me clarify how that works... Everything you know formed your attitude, which dictated your actions, which produced your results, which created your lifestyle—what your life actually looks, acts, and feels like right now.

Let me put it another way: What you learned, combined with what you believed about what you learned, ultimately determined what you thought. What you thought was responsible for the actions (or inactions) you took. Your actions (or inactions) produced your results, which in turn created your lifestyle—just as that same series of events created mine.

So if it's true—that what we know ultimately trickles down to how we live—what then is the best way to live an extraordinary life? The answer is simple. Get around the right people. Hang out in the right places. Learn the right stories. To further illustrate, let me share with you seven chronological examples of how this "getting around the right people, places, and stories" thing actually worked for me—and how it will work for you...

Who knew so many years ago that Tom Hopkins was the right person, that Portland, Oregon was the right place, and *How To Master The Art of Selling Anything* was the right story?

Who knew a few years later Chuck Crocker was the right person, his corner office was the right place, and *The Greatest Salesman in the World* was the right story?

Who knew a few years later Randy Gage was the right person, the SeaTac Marriott was the right place, and what he shared that afternoon was the right story?

Who knew a few years later John Milton Fogg was the right person, Upline® Journal was the right place, and Richard Poe knew how to tell the right story?

Who knew a few years later Jeff Olson was the right person, The Peoples Network was the right place, and a few of the speakers assembled therein knew how to tell the right story?

Who knew a few years later Orjan Saele was the right person, Oslo, Norway was the right place, and what I discovered in Scandinavia was the right story?

And who knows... Right now I might be the right person, you might be in the right place, and the book you now hold in your hands might indeed be the right story.

Remember, your lifestyle will continue to be directly linked to your awareness, thoughts, and actions. True, I somehow managed to get around the right people, places, and stories—and yet it was what I *did* with those events in my life that made all the difference. Therefore, read the following 24 stories, again, and again, and again; think about what you are learning; and apply these already proven principles to your business, and to your life. Because when you do, you will build a better business, ultimately design a better life...and who knows, along your way you too may become the right person, place, and story for someone else.

All the best,

MSC

P.S. Now allow me to share with you a story about activity, three rules of three, and one seemingly overlooked shortcut to success...

1.

ACTIVITY MATTERS MOST
YOUR SIMPLE SHORTCUT TO SUCCESS

Surveys have always fascinated me... Ask a few hundred people how they feel about this or that, and you can presumably understand the mindset of an entire nation! Indeed, polls are conducted daily to determine how we feel about politics, why we purchase certain products, and even what we watch—or don't watch—on TV.

All of this sampling got me thinking one day about this Network Marketing business we're in... For example, if you were to survey those already in the business, what would you ask them? What insights should they provide? And could any of this gleaned information be valuable to you?

Consider the following, and then decide...

Years ago I discovered that those who are deemed to be Masters in this "Networking thing" understand three simple truths about the business. Although you might hear these truths expressed somewhat differently from leader to leader, the underlying facts remain the same. For purposes of our discussion, we'll refer to these truisms as, "Network Marketing's Three Rules of Three."

1) Know the Business You're In

Network Marketing is about three things:
a) Finding people to talk to–Prospecting.
b) Talking to the people you find–Presentation.
c) Teaching others to do the same–Duplication.

2) Understand the Rules

Regardless of how you present your business:
a) Some people decide to join–Some will.
b) Some people decide not to join–Some won't.
c) Some people decide not to decide–So what...

3) Get Better at the Game

Because everything in life is about who you become:
a) Work more on yourself than you do on your business.
b) Again, work more on yourself than you do on your business.
c) And again, work more on yourself than you do on your business.

I share this with you because for years leaders have been searching for a simple, highly duplicatable system that new distributors could use to more quickly achieve success. And the most interesting part is, I now believe we've been overlooking the obvious for decades...

If it's true that in order to grow the organization, we need to contact people, involve them and teach them—and we do... If it's true that Some Will, Some Won't, and So What are all good things—and they are... And if we really need to be working on ourselves—our personal development—more than we work on the business... Well then, what could possibly be this simple shortcut to success?

To find the answer, conduct your own personal poll.

Take your census of the top 25 successful leaders in your company. Call them, text message them, or e-mail them—whatever it takes for you to get together long enough to ask three questions:

1) How were you introduced to the business—audiotape or CD, videotape or DVD, or through some event?

2) How would you describe the skill-set of the person who sponsored you?

3) Once you were introduced to the company, how long did it take to decide you wanted to do this business?

That's it!

And in case you're interested, here's what I've

discovered...

Question #1 could easily provide you with 25 different answers, especially if you ask which audiotape or CD, videotape or DVD, or event they attended. Question #2 again, will probably provide a plethora of answers from talented to tolerable to terrible.

Question #3 however, is the all-important key to your survey.

Because what the answers to this third question will reveal, are that leaders who make the most money in our industry—regardless of how they were introduced, and regardless of by whom—for some unexplained reason they "got it" and they "got in" right away... Those who build the largest organizations— same thing—they "got it" and they "got in" right away. And best of all (pay close attention here, because this is your simple shortcut to success) those you have yet to meet, those unnamed individuals destined to become leaders, they'll "get it" and "get in" right away too— almost regardless of what you know, say, and do—if you will just expose them to your business!

Imagine that! Activity matters most!

The beauty of this overlooked shortcut to success is knowing that in the beginning what you lack in skill, you can actually make up for with activity! Combine that belief with a proven system for contacting new prospects, and your company's next great "Triple Diamond Star Fleet Commander" could easily be sponsored by you—again, regardless of your current level of expertise!

Now I'm not suggesting that you skip mastering "Network Marketing's Three Rules of Three." Quite the contrary. Just because those fortunate few movers and shakers "got it" and "got in" right away, is no reason to miss sponsoring the masses who want to know everything about everything before they're ready to begin...

"...in the beginning what you lack in skill, you can actually make up for with activity!"

Therefore, if you truly desire to prosper long-term in this business, immediately begin to weave the golden thread of activity throughout your business tapestry—known to all successful leaders as "Network Marketing's Three Rules of Three"—and not only will you have an excellent chance of sponsoring that next mega superstar—you'll be able to keep them.

So what are you waiting for? Get something about your company—product, service, or opportunity— into the hands of your friends, family, and business associates right away....

"Network Marketing is about finding people to sponsor, sponsoring the people you find, and teaching those you involve how to do the same."

2.

MASTERING THE MUSIC
LEARNING IT ALL ONE VERSE AT A TIME

I attended the Rod Stewart concert in Seattle. Fabulous production! Amazing, that after all those years Rod can still electrify an audience. True, center seats in the eighth row did help... That's where everyone should sit... Close enough to see the color of the entertainer's eyes.

The show had ended—or so everyone thought... You should have seen that place. Ten thousand fans on their feet; clapping, cheering, and yes, occasionally screaming for their idol of the night to return and perform just one more song. As the seconds slowly turned into minutes, the acoustical accolades only increased. Apparently we were going to convince Rod Stewart and his band to return for an encore, or we were going to go deaf trying.

Then it happened. With the reinvigorated energy that only teenagers seem to possess, all eleven band members reappeared. And just when I was convinced this magical evening couldn't get any better—it did! Before the solo musician's mandolin melody could send a chill all the way up my spine, memory had already located the words...

Maggie May.

One of Stewart's classic mega hits from the 1970's. It had been decades since I had first fallen in love with that song, and years since I remembered hearing it... Yet as the music triggered some mental lyrical flood, I, and all the people around me, found our minds saturated with every verse...

> *"You master the words by hearing the music one more time."*

"Wake up Maggie, I think I've got something to say to you. It's late September, and I really should be back at school." Rod turned his microphone towards the audience. We sang. The band continued to play. And the only thing emerging from the Scotsman's mouth was a smile.

Can you imagine what that must feel like for an entertainer? Witnessing a sea of people, possessing but one voice. All having mastered the music, without ever having studied the words.

Perhaps that reality isn't so far-fetched. After all if your Network Marketing business consisted of ten thousand enthusiastic performers, I think we could agree that would be a good start.

So how about you? Do you know all the words? What about the distributors on your team? How do so many people master the music, without studying the words? As business-builders these are interesting questions to ponder. And in case you're wondering, I've been thinking about this for some time now. Here's what leaders know...

You master the words by hearing the music one more time.

Just as I fell in love with, and effortlessly memorized yet another piece of that song each time it played, you too can learn almost everything you need to succeed in Network Marketing by listening to the music over and over and over again.

So where is the music being played? On great audio programs, like the ones listed on the resource pages in the back of this book; at your weekly business briefings, as well as regional, national, and international conferences. For those who are tuned-in, the music is playing everywhere!

And here's the best part. By listening to these programs, and attending these events, you will magically learn the words. Words to best present your business. Words to encourage your new distributor. Words to grow your empire...

One example of this "mastering the words by hearing the music one more time" principle would be by attending each and every weekly business briefing. Successful business-builders understand this, and the three reasons they attend these events are:

1) To see it again.
2) To associate with others in the business.
3) To provide the proper environment for guests.

If you will immerse yourself in your business by attending every event for the next 12 months— including the event after the event—you will be amazed at what you will learn. And if you can convince those in your business to join you in that endeavor, you'll be well on your way to mastering the music, becoming a leader among leaders, and enjoying life the way it was meant to be....

3.

THE SEVEN TRUTHS
BUILDING YOUR LIFE OF MAGNIFICENCE

A wise man once defined success as a refined study of the obvious. How true. Most of what we need to know, say, and do to achieve mastery in Network Marketing could be easily taught—and understood—by a 12-year old.

Why then are we making this business so difficult?

Let's agree to start teaching *The Seven Truths* of Network Marketing to those who actually want to create their own destiny, and leave the rest of the world alone. After all, we're involved in a great industry, with wonderful people, offering unprecedented opportunity. And we should be proud to speak the truth...

1) Network Marketing is a business.

Networking is a unique form of enterprise, and you've got to understand the game you're playing.

Therefore, mentally consume every page of your distributor manual, online or the day it arrives. Listen to your audio training programs again, and again, and again. Like a song on the radio, you master the words by hearing the music one more time.

2) Freedom by the numbers.

Understand the numbers, and your compensation plan. Start by involving three or five people—whatever number of legs and leaders your plan dictates—and go to work. By your fifth year, the commissions paid on your invested efforts could well equal a mid six-figure annual income. After that, the sky's the limit.

3) Attend every live event.

The weekly presentation is part of the process. You need to be in attendance every week—to see the presentation again. Remember the music? You need the association, and the environment to showcase your company for your prospects. True, not everyone attending every meeting earns $10,000 a month. However, everyone earning $10,000 a month attends every meeting. Now that's a refined study of the obvious.

4) Work only one company.

Leaders understand this truth, because no man or woman can serve two masters.

5) Have a compelling, written "Why?"

Success in Network Marketing is 20% how to, and 80% why to... The best part is, if your reasons are strong enough you'll learn everything you need to know along your journey.

> *"Decide in writing you'll be here a year from now."*

6) Invest in yourself first.

Some people are trying to earn an exceptional wage, using an ordinary education. It can't be done. If you want to earn more, you've got to learn more. Therefore, read all the books, attend all the classes, and learn everything you possibly can.

7) Decide in writing you'll be here a year from now.

Long-term written goals possess the power to pull you right to the top of your company. Put your dreams for your future on paper, and begin building your life of magnificence.

The great Winston Churchill once said, "The truth is incontrovertible. Malice may attack it and ignorance may deride it, but in the end, there it is." *The Seven Truths.*

"*If you want this thing to work, you've got to work this thing you want.*"

4.

REPLAYING WHAT WORKS
FOCUSING ON WHAT YOU DO RIGHT

I ran across an interesting little distinction that, when fully understood and properly applied, will forever change the way you think, act, and teach the art of building your business.

Interested? Thought you might be...

It all started when Paul J. Meyer, a worldwide icon in the personal development industry, authored a fabulous book entitled, *Bridging The Leadership Gap* and was kind enough to send me an autographed copy...

Contained in this masterpiece, Paul shares his wisdom, along with a short story so profound, it simply must be retold.

Paul writes, "To develop your potential for effective leadership, begin with the strengths and abilities you

Michael S. Clouse

already possess. [Because] you are always stronger when you keep your successes and strengths in mind."

Driving home his point, Paul continues, "Vince Lombardi, who coached two teams to World Championships, observed that when football games were over, it always seemed that errors got more attention than successes. The newspaper and television media would highlight, analyze, and discuss the mistakes. One day, Lombardi decided, 'From now on, we are only going to replay our winning plays.' And look what happened to him and his team—his theory worked!"

"What would happen if you were to only focus on what you did right?"

Only replay our winning plays... Interesting concept.

How about you? What plays are you running over, and over, and still over again on that all too familiar screen inside your head?

What would happen if you were to only focus on what you did right? If you were to only replay those presentations that worked? If you were to only recognize your successes, and then repeat those accomplishments again, and again, and again? What might happen to your attitude, to your business, and to your life?

These are fascinating questions to ponder...

Leaders also understand, we must get back to the basics once every year. Echoing this, recall Vince Lombardi's most famous quote... His team had already won the World Championship. So how did training camp begin the following summer? Lombardi gathered his men together, and to his World Champions—with pigskin in hand—uttered his now immortal words, "Gentlemen, this is a football."

Indeed.

So what would this, "Getting back to the basics, with a focus on what you're doing right!" look like for your business? Well, because at its essence Network Marketing is about three things, it might look something like this:

1) Prospecting—You've got to find 'em.
2) Presentation—You've got to sponsor 'em.
3) Duplication—You've got to teach 'em how to do the same.

Therefore, acquire the knowledge, apply the skills, and teach everyone on your team how to do the same. Focus on what you do right. Repeat.

Now that's replaying what works... A simple formula for success anyone can follow.

*"Stop worrying about the person who says 'No.'
Focus instead on those who simply 'Don't know.'"*

5.

THE CLOUSEIAN FORMULA™
SIMPLIFYING THE UNIQUENESS OF SUCCESS

I've got this idea for a book and I wanted to share it with you... The working title is, *How To Build Your Network Marketing Business In Three Easy Steps*.

This idea came to me after a conversation with my son Taylor, who at the time was a junior in high school. Taylor was demonstrating his newest toy, a TI-92 graphics calculator, trying to teach 'Dad' how to 'simplify the expression,' which basically refers to how someone would reduce a complex mathematical problem to its simplest form.

I watched as Taylor entered the data into the TI-92... $\frac{(x^{-3}y^2)^{-4}}{(y^6x^{-4})^{-2}}$ ...pressed a few buttons and presto— out came the simplified solution x^4y^4. And I got it! No, not the math... For the first time I understood the solution to one of the most complex and misunderstood problems in our industry: Answering that elusive and frequently asked question, "How do I succeed in

Network Marketing?"

Let's face it... We all realize defining success is difficult *because* it means different things to different people. Everyone's answer is varied to some extent— and that can be really confusing. While some say, "Do this, and you'll achieve success." Others reply, "No, do it this way, because it only works this way." And still others retort, "Hey, everything works, so do whatever you want." More than a bit puzzling for someone trying to figure out this Network Marketing success thing.

And yet by not reducing success to its simplest form, too many of us are missing out on the answer— missing out, I believe, on a relatively simple formula that could work for every person, every time.

Is this really possible? Well, take a look at what I've come up with and decide for yourself...

If we reduce success in Network Marketing to its simplest form, the math looks like this:

$$s = (d + g + a)i^2$$

Translation: <u>s</u>uccess is achieved when you add together a burning <u>d</u>esire, written <u>g</u>oals, and consistent <u>a</u>ctivity, and then multiply that mixture with self-<u>i</u>mprovement squared (squared because the books you read, the CDs you hear, and the classes you take create a powerful synergistic effect over time). Wow! *The Clouseian Formula*™ actually acknowledges the uniqueness of success—and shows you how to achieve it!

And if you're not crazy about the math, consider the formula this way: look at the areas in your life you have the strongest __d__esire to alter, change, or improve. Next, prioritize your desires into written short-term and long-term __g__oals... Then, have someone help you select the right __a__ctivity-driven plan necessary to achieve all that you desire—and take immediate action... And as you move toward your desired goals, simultaneously go to work on getting a little better every day (all that self-__i__mprovement stuff I mentioned earlier) so that your journey becomes a little easier over time. Remember to celebrate your __s__uccess when it happens... Repeat!

"The Clouseian Formula™ *actually acknowledges the uniqueness of success—and shows you how to achieve it!"*

You see, successful business-builders understand that Network Marketing has always been, currently is, and will continue to be about self-improvement. Because in this industry, it's not what you get that's ultimately important—it's who you become in the process. And if that's true, then *your* success—and ultimately who you become—is as easy to define (and achieve) as: $s = (d + g + a)i^2$

So use the math, and write down what you truly desire to achieve, set some goals, and then go to work. Focus about an hour a day on the the $\underline{i}^2$ portion of the formula by asking yourself what skills you want to improve: prospecting, presentation, or duplication? Then pick up a book, listen to a CD program, or sign up for a class. Apply what you learned, and continue repeating this process: $s = (d + g + a)i^2$ until your life is working out just the way you planned.

How To Build Your Network Marketing Business In Three Easy Steps. Hey, maybe I'll write that book after all... However until I do, let's teach everyone, *The Clouseian Formula*™.

6.

THE 90-DAY SUCCESS CYCLE
BUILDING A BUSINESS THAT LASTS

All life operates on some sort of cycle... The changing of the seasons, from spring to summer to fall to winter, and then back to spring again every year. The phases of the moon... The rise and fall of the tides... And the way your Network Marketing business will be built. Indeed, in Network Marketing we too have a constant and predictable cycle we need to follow.

Let's review that cycle, keeping in mind as we do that our number one goal is to keep the main thing the main thing. And what is the main thing? Simply this: How many times today will your company's story be told by you, by one of your distributors, by a 3rd-party tool, or by an event? Learn to track that, and you can build a financial wall around your family that nothing can get through.

So what is *The 90-Day Success Cycle* and how

should you be using it to your advantage?

The 90-Day Success Cycle looks like this:

1) Your daily appointments feed into your home meetings, business luncheons, or other small events.

2) Your twice-weekly home meetings, business luncheons, or other small events, feed into your weekly business briefings.

3) Your weekly business briefings feed into your still larger monthly trainings.

4) Your monthly trainings feed into your quarterly regional, national, or international conferences.

5) Your quarterly regional, national, or international conferences complete *The 90-Day Success Cycle*, after which the cycle is repeated again....

Let's put some numbers to this, and then discuss the physiology behind the numbers. Then we'll review the single most important element of *The 90-Day Success Cycle:* Taking inventory.

If we were to add numbers (or people) to the five above-mentioned steps, it might look something like this:

1) Your daily appointments include you, your prospect, and (perhaps) your workout partner—for a maximum of three people. These presentations are 12 – 15 minutes in length, and are designed to advance your

prospect to the next events. Your daily appointments feed into your twice-weekly home meetings, business luncheons, or other small events...

2) Your twice-weekly meetings include you, two to ten guests, and your workout partner (or someone to give the presentation) for a maximum of twelve people. These presentations are about 30 – 45 minutes in length, and are designed to enroll your prospects, or to further your prospects' interest in attending your next event—as some prospects may still want more information. Your twice-weekly home meetings, business luncheons, or other small events, feed into your larger weekly business briefings...

3) Your weekly business briefings would include distributors within a 30 – 45 minute drive, and are typically held in a hotel, or conference room, on Monday, Tuesday, Wednesday, or Thursday evening. Again, you should attend these events for three reasons: to see the presentation again, for the association, and to provide the right environment for sponsoring guests. These weekly business briefings would include you, the prospects you invite, plus 10 – 250+ other distributors and their guests—creating an average briefing of between 25 – 250+ people. These formal presentations are 60 minutes in length, and designed to enroll your prospects. Your weekly business briefings feed into your still larger monthly trainings...

4) Your monthly trainings should include all distributors within a four hour drive, be conducted

by as many local leaders as you can fit on the agenda, and usually include an out-of-town expert, leader, or keynote speaker. These trainings cover the basics of the business, and may include between 100 – 1,000+ distributors. Your monthly trainings feed into your quarterly regional, national, or international conferences...

5) Your quarterly conferences complete *The 90-Day Success Cycle*, after which the process is then repeated.

"The main reason you hold an event is to promote the next event."

These events are usually sponsored by key leadership, and/or your Company, and include 2,000+ distributors, over a two-day period of time— requiring most distributors to travel 1,000 miles or more from their homes. The reason you attend these regional, national, or international conferences, is to transform yourself from "being in the business" to "the business being in you." This emotional transformation is what secures your financial future.

Now here are a few thoughts on taking inventory... After every major event you probably have a 90-day window of time until your next major event. This is the time to call all your key distributors and inquire: 1) Are they planning to attend the next major event? 2) What title do they want to achieve by the next conference?

3) How many distributors will be joining them at the next major event?

Building A Business That Lasts

1) Work in 90-Day cycles. Enough said...

2) Understand your prospecting and sponsoring success is simply the result of providing your prospects with multiple exposures over a short period of time.

3) The main reason you hold an event is to promote the next event. And you should attend every event.

4) Get to an event of 2,000+ distributors, held over a two-day period of time, 1,000 miles away, as soon as possible. Because, again, this will help to create the emotional transformation that will secure your financial future.

5) Take inventory after every major event, and then repeat *The 90-Day Success Cycle*.

And yet, when all is said and done, you must continue to ask yourself, "Am I keeping the main thing the main thing?" And what is the main thing? Simply this: How many times today will your company's story be told by you, by one of your distributors, by a tool, or by an event? Learn to track that, and you can build a financial wall around your family that nothing can get through.

"Success is when you have what you want.
Happiness is when you love what you have."

7.

INSTANT EVERYTHING
IT'S TIME WE STOP THE INSANITY

Man stands in front of that rectangular shaped, nuclear-particle device some call a microwave, mumbling under his breath, "Come on, come on, why is this thing taking so long?" All I can do is shake my head, and wonder if anyone ever informed our got-to-have-it-yesterday guy the reason we call it a lunch hour?

Well, the lunch hour is one thing, but now this "instant mentality" has found its way into Network Marketing. And what's worse is more than a few distributors have bought into this "Get rich overnight! I did. So can you!" ridiculously misguided belief.

Personally, aren't you a bit tired of all the half-truths, exaggerations, and lies being perpetuated in our industry? And yet, we see them every day—hundreds of unsolicited e-mails, countless ads in opportunity seekers magazines, and even the occasional postcard all promising instant riches and no downline to build because they will do all the work for you! Just complete the simple online application—include your credit card number to cover your required sucker fee—sit back and relax. Easy Street here you come!

Let me give you three examples of what I mean. Now keep in mind that these are actual Network Marketing ads taken from several different sources:

- HUGE INCOME! $10,000 1st month! I did. So can you. (800) 775-XXXX, Extension #1853

- MLM BREAKTHROUGH! Downline built for you guaranteed! No fees or hassles. (800) 372-XXXX

- YOU CAN EARN CASH DAILY! Call (800) 820-XXXX! Then call (703) 368-XXXX

And on, and on, and on it goes. The promise of no work, massive income, and all with zero risk. What could be better than that?

How about the truth?

If you really want to build a long-term successful business in Network Marketing, this is what you will need to do:

a) Select the right company, and make a life-long commitment.

By the way, you'll know you're with the right company if you can answer with a resounding "Yes!" to these two questions: 1) If there weren't a business model attached to my company's product(s), would I be buying them? And, 2) If I made a purchase (again without an opportunity to profit) would I be so excited by the benefits received, that through casual conversation I would share my experiences with friends, family, and business associates?

b) Invest eight to ten hours per week, one Saturday per month, and one weekend per quarter over the next two to five years.

Follow your company's proven business plan (or system) and you should be able to replace your full-time income. After that, the sky's the limit. And if your company doesn't have a proven business plan, well, that would be a clue...

> *"...we sell more dreams than all our products, goods, and services put together!"*

c) Start sharing the business with your friends, family, and business associates.

Tell the story, show the plan, and then ask your prospects if they would like to start dreaming again. After all, successful business-builders know we sell more dreams than all our products, goods, and services put together!

Last and certainly not least, avoid anything, and anyone who offers you their 30-day shortcut to instant success, because if it doesn't take two to five years to build, it's not a business, it's a game and one you probably won't want to play for very long.

> *"The secret to your success is to do the common things uncommonly well."*

8.

CREATING YOUR MASTER PLAN
DESIGNING THE BUSINESS YOU WANT

We have all heard it, "Eight to ten hours per week, one Saturday per month, and one weekend per quarter—for two to five years." Referring, of course, to the investment of time—your time—needed to achieve success in Network Marketing.

And as important as it is for you to reach that elusive status called "success," I think it would be an equally good idea to know *what* you're actually striving for—and *why* you desire to achieve it.

To accomplish this, we'll need to begin with a little "futuring" as it's called, and move on from there. In this exercise, you'll start by listing the ten most important accomplishments you aspire to attain over the next twelve months. Make your list quickly—without giving it a lot of thought—that way you will bring to the surface those ideals that are truly important to you.

Always written in present-tense language, your "futuring" could look something like this:

I drive a black Crossfire.
I have more friends than I can count.
I have more money than I can spend.
People are always excited to meet me.
I read ten pages of a good book each day.
I listen to CDs during my automobile drive time.
I pay myself first, and invest 10% of my income.
I talk with two people today about my business.
My life is a masterpiece because I design it that way.

By the way, your list may look completely different. After all, this is your life, and you may design it any way you choose—and you do need to choose—or others will decide your future for you... It's true. Because the universe cannot operate in a vacuum, every detail you leave out will be filled in by someone else.

> "...every detail you leave out will be filled in by someone else."

Therefore, after you have placed the direction of your future on paper, begin *Creating Your Master Plan*. For this portion of your life, you will need a daytimer, or calendar of sorts—something you can use to record the details of your new destiny...

To accomplish this, you need to schedule your

year—months, weeks, days and yes, even hours. First, block out the commitments you have already made. This would include the hours you work a full- or part-time job, anniversaries, vacations, etc. Make sure you do this for the balance of the year.

Now take another look at each and every month, and see if you missed anything; like family time, company functions, seminars you are going to attend, special events you might have missed on the first go-around, or a little time to just relax.

Sadly, most people will never experience success, because they just let time go by—and it does go by—hoping against hope, that everything will somehow turn out okay. And then, before they realize it, life has passed them by. We have got to be better than that! Therefore, with all your priorities in place—written down in your planner—you can, perhaps for the first time, see how and where to invest in the future you really desire.

Write down the hours you have planned for your two-on-one appointments, follow-up calls, and business briefings. Remember to schedule time to do your prospecting and your personal development too. In other words, find, and then put in writing, the "Eight to ten hours per week, one Saturday per month, and one weekend per quarter—for the next two to five years."

Because if you will just do a little planning, and then take action—remembering to improve a little every day—within two to five years they will call you "successful" in more ways than one.

9.

DON'T ASK ME, I'M ALREADY IN
NETWORK MARKETING'S
PERFECT PROSPECTING TOOL

Prospecting... It's the name of the game! And most of us have invested countless hours in our never-ending quest for that elusive "perfect approach." Yes, it seems many of us are still searching for the "one-liner" that when properly given would transform even your most uninterested prospect into a marketing maven. After all, somewhere out there is the world's next Networking Superstar just waiting to be discovered.

So, if we agree that prospecting is "the name of the game," and if we can further agree that there is a lot more talent to be found...well then, I have a question for you. Why do we all seem to be contacting each other?

Now, don't tell me you've not had the pleasure of being "introduced to a new company" just to "get your professional opinion" on the hottest new program to come along since 3M inadvertently invented the post-it-note? Regardless of how long you've been involved in Network Marketing, your e-mail is probably full of these daily "offers," and for some time now I've been keeping track of the commonalties. Interested? Thought you might be...

So far, I've narrowed these solicitations down to two things they all had in common. All promised their opportunity was "the best" and they all acknowledged me as someone who's already in the business. The never-ending streams of e-mails, occasional telephone calls, and even the infrequent letters all have that same tone: Dear Colleague, Dear Professional, and sometimes even, Dear Network Marketer.

What's the deal here? Aren't these people aware that only three percent of us are involved in Network Marketing? And therefore, 97 out of every 100 people aren't already in? Wouldn't it make more sense for us to e-mail, call, or—here's a thought—actually go see the other 97 prospects?

So please—*Don't ask me, I'm already in!*

And about that line of wanting to only contact experienced people—well, I don't buy it... Because if you really wanted to sponsor someone who's already trained, why aren't you calling Triple Diamond Crown Ambassador Bill Britt, or Texas Networking legend Tom "Big Al" Schreiter, or Network Marketing company owner and Dean of Personal Development

Richard Brooke? These people are trained, polished and wouldn't require much of your time. Of course, you would need to spend the rest of your life just trying to sponsor them.

You know, there's got to be a better way to introduce the beauty and power of Network Marketing to all those millions of outsiders, and I think I've got it! What if we all wore buttons like the ones Herbalife® made popular in the '80s? You remember: "Lose Weight Now, Ask Me How." Only with a different slogan. That way, we would all know who to approach and who to skip.

"Don't Ask Me, I'm Already In"

It's simple, to the point, and who knows, maybe it will even start a conversation that allows you to sponsor your next superstar.

"If you will become the very best messenger you possibly can, the message will take care of itself."

10.

27 PROSPECTS LATER
A NEVER-ENDING SOURCE OF NEW LEADS

Sadly, it is often the most common story told in our business...

It seems "Mary" had been in four different deals (and I'm using the word—"deals"—correctly) before finding the Network Marketing Company of her dreams. The problem: Mary is trying to put together yet another warm market list—a list of at least 100 people for her to contact.

Warm market indeed! As our fictitious friend stares down at her yellow lined blank sheet of paper, she now understands what it feels like to be an official member of the NFL club—No Friends Left!

Frustrated with the knowledge that she has no one to contact, and with her sights still set on success, Mary heads straight towards a cold cruel market—that wild wintry world of advertising, cold calls and worst of all, those opportunity seekers' e-mail lists.

With no degree in marketing, no advertising experience, and without any knowledge of the right prospecting tools, our friend Mary is doomed to fail. And the saddest part is, she will probably blame her downfall on our industry, her new company, or a lack of upline support.

But what if there was a better way?

Well, there is...

Years ago I discovered a great way to create a never-ending source of new prospects while I was attempting to reserve a booth at a local trade show. Unfortunately, I was a little late and the show had already sold out. Interested in learning all I could, I decided to go anyway, do a little research and determine if the next event would prove a profitable possibility.

"If you want more prospects, set aside four hours, grab 10 bucks and your business cards, and check out an appropriate trade show in your area."

My goal was simple: Enter each booth, ask to speak with the person in charge, and start the conversation off letting them know I had tried to reserve space in the show, but it had already sold out. I asked them about the show: "Was this the first time they had exhibited here? Were the attendees just looking or were they buying?"

Then it hit me: What if, after a few questions and

some general rapport building, I asked this question: "Do you think my company would do well at a show like this?"

"I don't know," would come their seemingly scripted reply, followed by an apparently pre-programmed, "What does your company do?"

Bingo! Got 'em! Hook, line and sinker—along with the chance to give my 30-second commercial 100 times in four hours. This was better than having a booth (and cheaper, too). Twenty-seven prospects later, I'd perfected the system. And, I might add, it has been working beautifully for years.

If you want more prospects, set aside four hours, grab 10 bucks and your business cards, and check out an appropriate trade show in your area. Using this approach, you'll walk away with all the hot leads you can handle.

And if you're interested in learning a few more great ways to prospect, get your hands on a copy of, *Seven Prospecting Secrets.* Send your e-mail request to: secrets@nexera.com. We'll make sure you receive a free copy.

"In Network Marketing, duplication is what success looks like."

11.

How To Effectively Tell Your Story
What Every Prospect Needs To Hear

When you stop to think about it, every weekly business briefing—and every large event—needs to include powerful, effective testimonials (or what I call stories), somewhere during the presentation, for the benefit of both distributors and new guests alike.

So how can you ensure that you're ready to contribute with your powerful and effective stories? Consider putting into practice the following four-point plan:

1) Every distributor needs to create his or her own story (testimonial) regarding the product or service, and the money.

2) Write it down. Your story should include: your name, where you live, your background or occupation, followed by your product, or money story.

3) Practice, drill, and rehearse the words you've written until you can cover every point in 30 – 45 seconds.

4) When it comes to your money story, I would suggest converting your money story into your lifestyle story... After all, why would someone who is already earning $10,000 per month want to join your business? Because of the lifestyle!

Not fighting the traffic is lifestyle.
Being home with your kids is lifestyle.
Doing work that brings you satisfaction is lifestyle.
Waking up after you're finished sleeping is lifestyle.

Instead of earning $500 in your home-based business, ask yourself "What am I doing with the $500?" And if your answer is that you are buying back some of your life—for example, the ability to retire at 55 instead of retiring at 65—that's lifestyle!

What sounds more impressive? "I earn $700 per month in my home-based business..." or "With the extra money our business provides, we were able to take another two-week dream vacation in the middle of February to Aruba!"

Take the time to prepare both your product and lifestyle stories. Write them down and practice both until you know them—like you know your own name. Then make sure you inform your local leadership team that you've got two powerful and effective stories, and you're ready to let the world know....

Creating Your Story

Keep your story to 30 – 45 seconds!

Your goal is to relate, relate, relate, to as many people as possible.

Include: your name, your location, your background, how you were introduced to the business, or why you decided to become a distributor, and what your business has done (or is doing) for you... Remember relate, relate, relate!

Example: "My name is Michael Clouse... My wife and I have two grown children and live in Seattle. Prior to becoming a distributor with the XYZ Company, I had gone from an Account Executive position with AT&T, to Editor-in-Chief of a business magazine, to a small business owner... And then

> *"Take the time to prepare both your product and lifestyle stories."*

this home-based business just kind of fell in my lap. Well, I took a look, liked what I saw, got involved, and using the system they taught me, went to work on a very part-time basis... Today, just a few short years later, I earn over $100,000 a year, my wife and I just spent three-weeks in Italy, and I'm still only working part-time! I guess you could say that getting involved with this business continues to be one of the best decisions I have ever made." A total of 38 seconds!

This story relates to: Seattle, married, children, family, white collar worker, salesperson, technology, journalism, small business owner, there is a system you can follow, part-time, six-figure income, travel, vacations, this was the right decision, time freedom.

Because if you would just take a few minutes and complete this simple and yet extremely vital aspect of your business, and then teach this to all those on your team, you will keep more distributors excited about the possibilities, and sponsor more guests too....

12.

SALES VS. THE SYSTEM
BECOMING A BETTER MESSENGER

Yes, I know to some of you, this is about sales... And I understand the points you probably are making right now. Still, I have a real problem with all this "sales" stuff.

Why? I'm glad you asked.

Selling is an art and a profession all its own. Selling is a learned set of skills that may take years to perfect. Tom Hopkins teaches, "No woman, in a delivery room, ever gave birth to a salesperson." And back in 1979, when I first attended his *How to Master the Art of Selling* seminar, I became a serious believer! Salespeople aren't born great. Salespeople are made great!

So what's the big deal? Why not just master the art of selling, and be done with it? Well, it's not that simple...

Let me explain what I mean by asking you two questions. First: What is the "one thing" that you do better than anything else?

Okay. Next question: How long did it take you to achieve the skills necessary to become as excellent as you currently are doing that "one thing" you currently do so well?

Really? That long?

Are you beginning to understand the problem?

When I decided to become a maven at this selling game, I went back to school and studied—for years. Xerox's Professional Selling Skills I, II & III...been there, done that. Zig Ziglar, Roger Dawson, Tony Robbins, Brian Tracy...and on, and on, and on! Year after endless year, course after never-ending course...and those are just a few of the better-known classes. I won't even begin to mention all the First Interstate Bank seminars (used to work there), or the AT&T events (worked there too), I attended over the last 25+ years.

> "Finding people to sell and then selling the people you find isn't duplicatable. And in Network Marketing, it doesn't really work long-term."

Now, don't get me wrong. It's not that I didn't enjoy the process. To the contrary—I loved every minute of it! To this day the walls of my home office are filled with certificates, plaques and trophies; and like you, I'm very proud of my accomplishments. The problem is that learning, or worse yet, teaching someone how to sell isn't something that you or I can easily duplicate. And isn't that what we are trying to accomplish in Network Marketing? Aren't we attempting to create—or follow—a system that anyone can utilize? Of course we are...

Finding people to sell and then selling the people you find isn't duplicatable. And in Network Marketing, it doesn't really work long-term.

We're all much better off sponsoring people who have a burning desire to change their own lives and then plugging them into a system (using 3rd-party tools) that will allow them—regardless of their background—to succeed at any level they truly desire.

So if the above is true—and it is—as successful business-builders, what should we be doing? Frankly, we would all be better served if we focused more on learning a duplicatable system, and less on perfecting our closing skills.

As one wealthy Network Marketer once put it, "If you will become the very best messenger you possibly can, the message will take care of itself." Indeed it will....

"*This business is not about 'getting them in,'*
it's about 'keeping them in.' And they're not
'in' until they're involved."

13.

FIVE WAYS TO HEAT UP YOUR COLD DISTRIBUTORS
BECAUSE NOTHING HAPPENS UNTIL SOMETHING HAPPENS

Water has always fascinated me. Freeze it, thaw it out and watch it return to its original form. Liquid to solid to liquid once again... Now try that with an egg!

Indeed, this wonderfully refreshing "two parts hydrogen one part oxygen" nutritional chaser is incredible stuff.

For example, did you know that water never freezes at exactly 32 degrees? It's true. And here's the amazing part—ice at 32 degrees will never thaw! Seems as though water is in some sort of suspended animation at 32 degrees.

Ever have any distributors stuck at 32 degrees? You know, the ones who attend your business briefing every week and never bring a guest? They're in, and yet not in-terested enough to do anything. They don't quit, and yet they don't work the business either. They just seem, well, suspended at 32 degrees...

I'm not sure if Yogi Berra, the great New York Yankee's manager, knew about this 32 degree thing when he said, "Nothing happens until something happens." But I'll bet even Yogi faced this same dilemma with his players...

What do you suppose he did?

Although we'll probably never know for sure about Yogi, I have prepared a surefire way to heat up your 32 degree distributors. It's called, *The Sponsoring Rule of Five*. And if you're serious about your success, give it a try—because the results will astound you...

1) Only sponsor those people with whom you would like to become friends.

This is simple and to the point. After all, if you don't want them in your home, why would you want them in your business?

2) Invest your time with those you personally sponsor.

Get to know them for who they are, and for who they want to become. You should understand the circumstances, needs, and dreams of everyone you personally bring into the business.

3) Set up a game plan—and follow through.

Without the architectural blueprint, or plan, the building would not be built. And without your commitment to complete the task, event the smallest goal is wasted. Prepare a game plan with those you enroll, and then commit to partnering with them to achieve their desired end-result.

"Only sponsor those people with whom you would like to become friends."

4) Talk with those you sponsor every week.

Successful business-builders talk with their team. They're interested. And over time, this simple talking-with-your-team technique will have you doing business with those you know well.

5) Become close personal friends inside and outside the business.

People may choose to leave a business, but nobody chooses to leave a friend. Because Network Marketing is about creating a fabulous lifestyle, make sure you enjoy yours with those you sponsor along the way.

The Sponsoring Rule of Five... Now that's how to create some heat!

Michael S. Clouse

---

*"Leadership can only exist when people
are willing to follow."*

14.

THE DAILY 1/2 DOZEN THINGS
DESIGNED TO MAKE YOU A SUPERSTAR

I f it's true—and it is—that leadership can only
exist when people are willing to follow, we must
be asking ourselves, "Why would someone want
to follow me?" And the best answer is, because you're
doing, *The Daily 1/2 Dozen Things!*

So what are *The Daily 1/2 Dozen Things* that will
make 80% of the difference? Take a look...

Your Daily Activity

1) Using your personal success planner, focus on
your goals for 15 minutes each day! Know "where"
you're going and "why?"

2) Listen to 30 minutes of an audiotape or CD every
day! Remember to focus on: Prospecting—because
you've got to find 'em. Presentation—because you've
got to enroll 'em. And Duplication—because you've
got to turn 'em into leaders who can do the same.

Therefore, each month go to work on getting better in one area of your business.

3) Read ten pages of a good book every day. Remember if you can read and you choose not to, you are illiterate by choice! The "Your Library" link on nexera.com offers a great selection to choose from.

4) Expose two new prospects every day using a system anyone can duplicate (audio and video tapes, CDs and DVDs, e-mail and Website, two-on-one, or live event). And if you want to learn how to more quickly grow your empire, use the simple, proven, and extremely effective concepts taught on our best-selling audio program, *Your Prospecting Toolbox* available through nexera.com/ypt.

"Expose two new prospects every day—using a system anyone can duplicate."

5) Follow-up with your prospects... Get them "in" and then get them "involved!" Because if they see you as a successful business-builder—and as a friend—they will stay in the game even longer.

6) Follow through with your distributors—those you've perceived as potential leaders. Meet with them weekly for the first year—at the weekly events—and invest some quality one-on-one time with them as well. Because, again, this business is not about getting them in, it's about keeping them in... And they're not "in" until they're involved.

You don't need to work every day—but on the days you do work, these are the daily activities designed to make you a superstar. Remember: Easy to do! Easy not to do!

For the next three months, experience success by doing *The Daily 1/2 Dozen Things,* and watch your organization multiply.

"The basics are the business."

15.

YOUR APPROACH MARKET
BUILDING THE BUSINESS WHILE
LIVING YOUR LIFE

Regardless of the prospecting processes you now have in place, every distributor in every city in the world should be tapping into the vast potential of their local community on a daily basis... Why? Well, the citizens you meet at the grocery story, dry cleaner, and fitness center—aren't most of these people potential prospects for your products? And what about the individuals you see at your corner coffee house, family restaurant, and neighborhood shopping mall—aren't many of these people potential prospects for your business too? Of course they are...

So if you're ready to learn how to easily and affordably take advantage of this huge, ever-changing pool of new people to talk to, please read on... Because by utilizing, *Your Approach Market* you can easily create a daily method of operation that almost anyone can duplicate...

Now this technique does require a little pre-planning... First, acquire your company's best CD, or audiotape—product, business, or both; whatever offer or message you're looking to get into the marketplace—along with a simple brochure that complements the CD or audiotape presentation. Second, make sure you place a label on each CD or audiotape and brochure; which includes your name, contact number, along with your Website address if at all possible. Something simple like this will work just fine:

Mary Johnson
206-364-1890
www.mycompany.com/mjohnson

Third, take the CD or audiotape (with your label applied) and wrap the brochure (with your label applied here too) around it, and then secure everything with a rubber band.

Your Approach Market exposure is one of the easiest to do because it simply allows you to place an audio pack into the hands of someone you meet—your prospect—while you're out and about in everyday life... And best of all, the number of contacts you and a small team can make using this simple approach can be extraordinary!

If you will teach this simple daily method of operation to all those on your team, your business will certainly grow... After all if you, along with a small group of just 30 distributors, were to expose two people a day, five days a week—that would create 62 exposures a day; 310 exposures a week; 1,240 every month; 14,880 exposures in a year! So make sure you have the most current audio packs available, and enough on hand to complete the task!

Remember when working *Your Approach Market*—or any other market for that matter—to note that in this business, you are the messenger; the audio pack is the message. Therefore, only focus on what you can control—delivery of the audio pack... Because you will positively learn over time that

"If you will teach this simple daily method of operation to all those on your team, your business will certainly grow."

prospecting just two a day will bring freedom your way!

So whom should you approach, and what should you say? Well, when you leave your home each day just bring two audio packs with you, and as you go about your day, look for people you feel might be interested in what you're offering... It's that simple. When you meet someone at the store, dry cleaner, fitness center, corner coffee house, family restaurant, neighborhood shopping mall, or anyplace you happen to be, simply find a way to say hello, and begin a short conversation... Here are a few examples:

Look for sharp people (compliment them) and ask,

"Excuse me, do you know anyone, or of anyone, who would like to earn an extra $500 to $1,000 a month?" When they express an interest, hand them your audio pack, ask for a business card, and then follow-up...

To a business owner: "I'm a recruiter in the _____ industry... (compliment them) Tell me, are you keeping your business options open?" When they express an interest, hand them your audio pack, ask for a business card; and then follow-up...

To someone who gives you good service: "I'm a recruiter in the _____ industry... (compliment them) Tell me, are you keeping your career options open?" When they express an interest, hand them your audio pack, ask for a business card; and then follow-up...

When asked, "What company do you represent?" or "What do you do for a living?" respond with: "I represent..." followed by your 30-second benefit-driven "Why would this person want to get involved?" commercial. Hand them your audio pack, ask for a business card; and then follow-up...

When you expose two people a day remember to be yourself—the messenger—and let the message take care of itself. Your objective here is to bring the presentation to the people, then follow-up, and get those people to the next presentation.

Your Approach Market is truly a powerful way to develop two new prospects every day—right in your own backyard.

16.

Prospecting Inside the Organization

Being There When The Timing Is Right

Prospecting... It's the name of the game! And having so stated the obvious, prepare to discover yet another part of the solution. Because, *Prospecting Inside the Organization* is just a single technique and should, therefore, only be part of your overall "Where-am-I-going-to-find-'em?" strategy.

Before we begin let's agree that, *Prospecting Inside the Organization* recognizes these four points as truth:

1) You have a group of distributors that are already sponsored, some by you personally, and yet most of whom were brought into the business by someone else on your team.

2) As your business continues to grow, it becomes more difficult to personally know everyone in your downline... Therefore, your goal is to develop a core

leadership team of about 30 key distributors, and then to personally work with this ever-evolving group.

3) When it comes to building your business, sometimes the timing is wrong... Sometimes the timing is right! Your job is to be there, *Prospecting Inside the Organization* when the timing is right.

"Keep calling until you have two to four new people to work with."

4) The larger your business becomes, the more this statement is true: "At any given moment someone in your business will make a decision to actually do something with this business... to get started again." However, they may not even know how to get re-activated, or what they need to do in order to build a successful business.

So how does, *Prospecting Inside the Organization* actually work?

By incorporating the following four points, you can begin "finding" those who are already signed up in your business—the ones where the timing is now right—and immediately begin teaching them how to achieve their dreams!

1) Get a copy of your organizational printout in front of you, and be prepared to make a few calls.

2) Have a good reason to call: You want to develop your business in a certain city, state, or province. Perhaps you are looking for a certain organizational

structure for that next promotion...or if your business is small enough, you can simply call everyone.

3) Pick up the telephone, and give those you want to "prospect" a call. Let them know a) who you are: your name and the name of your company, and b) why you're calling. For example, they live in San Francisco, or Toronto, or Oslo, and you're looking to expand your business in that area. c) Explain why you're interested in them... You have achieved a certain level of success in this business, and you're looking for someone to partner with for the next 90 days. You came across their name on your company printout, and decided to give them a call to find out if d) they would be interested in personally working with you over the next 90 days to see what the two of you could accomplish together.

4) Keep calling until you have two to four *new* people to work with. Then treat 'em just like you would if you were personally bringing them on board. Schedule a getting-started game plan within 48 hours; teach them how to develop their list; help them schedule their time; suggest the books they should read, the audio programs they should listen to, and the classes they should attend, etc.

Because *Prospecting Inside the Organization* works, but only to the degree that you work it...

And if you really want to know what your current potential is, start counting the zeros next to all those names on your organizational report! Because after all at some past point they did actually sign up... And today, if they're not doing anything at all—your job is to contact them, find out if the timing is right, and then help them get started again!

By the way, if you have an e-mail list, this would be a great time to update it as well. Just remember, some won't be ready when you call, however with their e-mail address in hand, you can begin "dripping" on them again... And who knows, the next time you give them a call, the timing might be perfect!

17.

USING THE RIGHT WORDS
TRAINING, TEACHING, AND EDUCATING

Words have always fascinated me. Take, for example, the comparable expressions of education and training. Both basically intend the same thing and convey the equivalent idea—right? So could it really matter which you use when describing what you really mean to say?

Before you answer too quickly, let me ask you: Is there a distinction—perhaps even a fundamental difference—between sex *education* and sex *training?*

And if you're still thinking that what you say may not be as important as how you say it, consider enrolling your 16-year old daughter in that next sex training class!

By the way if you're interested, we train animals, teach children, and educate adults. Unless of course the adults are behaving like animals or children, in which case it does become a judgment call...

Michael S. Clouse

Let's face it—words do matter. Here's what I mean...

Over the last several years I've noticed—and I'm sure you have too—a certain language developing within our industry. A language much more DEstructive than CONstructive.

Some of the words being used to explain what we do are making our business appear tawdry and cheap... And if we're ever going to elevate our vocation to the highest level possible, there is a bit of vocabulary cleanup that I say (with words) we need to do.

With this in mind, let's all agree to upgrade the professionalism of our language as follows:

Incorrect	*replaced with*	Correct
Deal or Opportunity		Business
Program		Company
Recruit		Sponsor/Enroll
Residual Income		Ongoing Income
Pitch		Presentation
Marketing Plan		Compensation Plan
My Team		The Team
My Organization		The Organization

It's simple: We're not in a deal, we're in a business. The information you requested on my program becomes the information you requested on the Company. The Army recruits bodies, we sponsor, or enroll people. And using the word residual to denote your pay plan will get you into trouble quicker than you can say "Attorney General." Better we share all the benefits of ongoing income... Pitch belongs in baseball, not in your presentation. The marketing plan isn't how we market, it's how we are compensated, and therefore it's the compensation plan. And please understand that if you successfully teach every distributor on the team to use the word "my" to denote their business, they will be overseeing an organization of one—which is, of course, the loneliest number.

"...we train animals, teach children, and educate adults."

From this day forward let's choose our words wisely, and together we can continue to create an industry that we are all proud to represent.

"Confidence is preparation's twin."

18.

CHANGING YOUR BELIEFS

ACQUIRING ACCURATE KNOWLEDGE

I can still recall the conversation... My friend Tim had telephoned in a panic to ask, "What color is engine oil?"

I replied, "That depends. If you're asking about the color of new engine oil—somewhere between silky green and shiny brown. However, if you're asking about old oil—anywhere from dirty green to dull brown."

"Oh..." came Tim's somewhat surprised response. And then after pausing long enough to seemingly reflect on what I had said, he continued, "So why is mine bright red?" As it turned out, Tim—in a first attempt to change his own oil—had completely drained the transmission fluid from his truck! Not what he had intended at all...

What happened? Three things: 1) Tim believed he could change his oil. 2) Tim also believed he had the necessary tools to complete the job—wrench, drain pan, plus a few quarts of new engine oil he had picked up at the auto supply store. And perhaps the most important point of all: 3) What Tim *believed* was *wrong!* In fact, had he replaced the transmission drain plug, added five more quarts of oil, and started his engine—his actions, that sprang from what he thought he knew, would have cost him plenty!

So what about you? Ever been in a situation like Tim where you thought you knew the right course of action to take, and paid the price for some mistaken belief? And if you have, perhaps the real question you should be asking is, "How did I create my beliefs in the first place?"

> *"Your beliefs were initially created, then evolved or remained unchanged, based on your perception of reality."*

Once you understand how you came to think the way you do, you will also come to realize that in fact you too possess the wisdom to alter, adjust, or amend anything in your life you're not excited about— and that's a good thing!

With this in mind, let's examine how you acquired your beliefs in the first place by considering seven *huge* clues:

"For as he thinketh within himself, so is he..."
—Solomon

"The Vision that you glorify in your mind, the Ideal that you enthrone in your heart—this you will build your life by, this you will become."

—James Allen

"Human beings can alter their lives by altering their attitudes of mind."

—William James

"First comes thought... Then organization of that thought into ideas and plans. Then transformation of those plans into reality."

—Napoleon Hill

"Whether you think you can, or you think you can't—you're right."

—Henry Ford

"We become what we think about."

—Earl Nightingale

"Great thoughts reduced to practice become great acts."

—William Hazlitt

It's true... Every belief—right or wrong—was created (and can be changed) using the following five-step process:

1) You acquired accurate knowledge
2) You thought about that knowledge
3) You acted—or failed to act—upon that knowledge
4) You got results from your actions—or from your inactions
5) Your beliefs were initially created, then evolved or remained unchanged, based on your perception of reality

Therefore, if you truly want to adopt a new belief, acquire *accurate* knowledge, think on that knowledge, act on that knowledge, get better results because of that knowledge, and experience the awesome power of your mind!

19.

A Leader Must Know
What The Organization Is Doing

I attended a Network Marketing training the other day. A nice group of people who were, for the most part, just getting started in the business. The instructor seemed to know his material, and was a good presenter. In fact, everything was going along quite smoothly, until the incident...

Let me ask you a question. If you could design, and then create, the perfect organization of distributors, what would it look like? How large? How skilled? How duplicatable?

Duplicatable? Oh! There's that word again! Why is this concept of repeating an agreed upon methodology so vitality important to the long-term success of your enterprise? Let me explain...

It has been said, and rightly so, the only commonality all religions of the world share is *belief,* all asking you to consider as true things you may, or may not, fully understand and at times can't necessarily prove. Right or wrong, that's the way theology has worked. And your Network Marketing business should function pretty much that way too... Everyone singing from the same hymnal. Now that's not a bad idea.

Here's the problem: From a leadership perspective, our industry doesn't tend to attract drones. On the contrary; this form of entrepreneurial experience entices the motivated maven movers and shakers of the *J.O.B. Community*. And then, as soon as we've enrolled our newest potential superstars, we allow *them* to tell *us* how *they're* going to build the business. Who knows, perhaps that explains why we have but one true God, and so many different downlines!

How about you? How are you doing with this duplication thing? Fair? Average? Great? And based upon your answer, if there were a simple way to predict your Networking future, would you be interested in peering into the vast unknown? Because we all have two ways to view the future—one with anticipation, the other, with apprehension, I'll share the information, and leave the rest to you...

Go get a copy of your organizational printout—you know, the one your company provided after you'd signed your life away, and paid a small fee. Next, select one, two, or three individuals from each different level shown on your report. After highlighting these distributors—making sure you randomly choose some new, some old, some successful, some not—pick up the telephone and give them a call. After all, if they're in your business, getting to know them would be the right thing to do.

Introduce yourself, ask if they have a few minutes to speak with you, and let them know the reason for your call: you're conducting a little survey, and were hoping they could help you out. Find out how long they've been with your company, why they decided to enroll, their favorite product or service, and so on, and so forth.

What you ask is really dependent on what you would like to discover. However, I would suggest that you prepare your list of about ten questions, to avoid the possibility of winging it... And then somewhere along the way, shift your inquiry to the business structure. In essence, where are they finding prospects? How are they introducing the business? What CDs, DVDs, or brochures do they use? Are they attending the weekly events, etc.

"Even if the people and personalities are different, the principles and processes should be the same."

What you're looking for, of course, is "top to bottom, left to right, everyone being on the same page" commonality. Since we don't live in a perfect world, that probably will never be the case. However, you do need to discover if the overall system is in place. Even if the people and personalities are different, the principles and processes should be the same. Because in Network Marketing, duplication is what success looks like!

Back to my story—you remember, the incident... What this instructor went on to say in part was, "We are now going to conduct business a new way." That "new way" was not approved by corporate, and would, if implemented, eliminate upline, downline, and crossline, taking money out of other people's pockets, and potentially placing it directly into his... Not a good idea.

Luckily, this issue was quickly discovered, and immediately corrected. Which reminds me that over a lifetime, parents, and yes, even Network Marketing leaders, need to be asking, "Do I know what my children are doing?" Believe me, finding out is a better than great idea.

So, if you would like to improve your duplication, then get your printout, make the calls, and find out what everyone's up to... Armed with that information, seek the counsel of someone in your upline you respect, and then make the necessary adjustments. Because a leader must know what the organization is doing.

20.

RETURN TO OZ
YOU'VE ALWAYS HAD THE POWER

W e're off to see the Wizard... The wonderful Wizard of Oz... He truly is a wonderful Wiz, if ever a Wiz there was...

Seems "We're all off..." to find something. Searching for answers... Sometimes for people... Whatever it takes to get from where we are to where we want to go.

Dorothy just wanted to get back to Kansas. And, lest we forget, the friends she met along her way were searching too: for brains, a heart and courage.

The Wizard of Oz is a classic metaphor for leadership. Dorothy discovered that leadership begins with knowledge in action—"Just follow the yellow brick road"—and ends with the realization, "There's no place like home."

Because from time to time we all need to be reminded, that if we just stay the course, we will reach our goals. Yet, the real wizardry of Oz is more subtly intertwined throughout the movie.

Remember, Scarecrow believed he didn't have a brain, but he masterminded Dorothy's rescue. Convinced he was without a heart, the Tin Man tried, repeatedly, to contain his emotions. And when it mattered most, the Lion, still searching for courage, was absolutely fearless. Each one possessed exactly what he had been searching for all along.

"Because from time to time we all need to be reminded, that if we just stay the course, we will reach our goals."

And yet concealed in Oz's last scene is perhaps the greatest leadership lesson of all:

Dorothy: *Can you help me...*

Good Witch of The North: *You don't need to be helped any longer. You've always had the power to go back to Kansas.*

Dorothy: *I have?*

Scarecrow: *Then why didn't you tell her before?*

Good Witch of The North: *Because she wouldn't have believed me. She had to learn it for herself.*

Dorothy believed the Wizard had the power—turns out he was just the little man behind the curtain.

Dorothy had the Ruby Slippers—the real power—all along. And that's what true leadership is about. Helping people see their power, helping them bring out the greatness that was really there all along.

Because the dreams that you dare to dream really do come true...but only when you decide it's time to wake up and live them!

"Oh Auntie Em, it's you...."

> *"Work only with those you would choose as friends."*

21.

BUILDING RELATIONSHIPS
YOUR BEST INVESTMENT OF TIME

It's early Tuesday morning, and I haven't finished sleeping. Daylight streams in through the unfamiliar window above as I try to ignore its subtle power, but I am losing the battle. Caught up in a world not all that far removed from my own, I lie half awake anticipating the day in a back basement bedroom so warm and comfortable my body is unwilling to move.

We are to depart Kelowna at 8:00AM, a picture postcard town located somewhere along the 50th parallel in the heart of the Canadian Okanagan Valley. Long drive ahead of us. Have been told we are to travel by car over roads mostly of asphalt, sometimes gravel, and the occasional "you-have-got-to-be-kidding-me" dirt stretch destined to add a new rattle or two to even the most well-crafted vehicle.

Our final destination on this Network Marketing business trip is Fort St. John, B.C., Canada. Thirteen hundred kilometers, and 15 hours due north into an area of wilderness the locals affectionately call "The Bush." With bags packed for our five-day excursion stacked neatly throughout the van, a full tank of gas, and Amanda Marshall's, *Let it Rain* playing softly on the CD player, the journey, and our conversation begins...

We speak of philosophy, of life, and of its purpose. Also the books one must read, movies worth a second look, and review in detail the numerous worldwide destinations we should include along the way. Minute after minute. Hour followed by still endless hour, we have a chance to do what so few in this world seem able to do—really connect as people. To engage in endless dialogue, and by choice learn everything we possibly can about another human being.

If it's true that the three most important things you will ever leave to your children are your photographs, your personal journals, and your library, what then is your most prized possession while you are living? Complex question, perhaps, but with a simple answer—because nothing can be more valuable than your relationships.

Gazing out the passenger window a few hours into the day, our words come to an abrupt end. Stunned, we watch in amazement as six bald eagles perched upon the mighty limbs of an old cottonwood tree majestically survey the bend in the river below. I've never witnessed such a sight. The beauty that surrounds us is breathtaking. Our conversation continues...

If you really want to know someone, you must uncover his or her core values. Asking simple questions like, "What is most important to you in life?" Followed by the obvious, "What is important to you about that?" And the all-important clarifying question, "How will you know when you have it?"

Getting to know people for who they are is what we should do best. Sadly, as entrepreneurs we rarely develop our relationship skills as carefully as needed for that. As business leaders, it's time we start understanding this fundamental point. As the chain breaks at its weakest link, so, too, your enterprise will rust and decay wherever it is least attended.

> *"The next time you decide to develop a leader, begin your journey by becoming a friend."*

Therefore, we must make time, and really get to know those in our lives for who they are, and for the individuals they wish to become. This is good for business. This is good for life.

Along our journey we wait for a herd of elk to cross the road before continuing; almost hit a bear... we count deer, a coyote, and one red-tailed fox. The Bush, and our lives, are amazing places—a collection of experiences, and their intensity.

And while some may selectively choose to recall only the rain, unpaved roads, and the Fort St. John mud, we prefer a pizza parlor in Jasper, photographing a lake in the warm afternoon sunshine, and over thirty hours of endless conversation—building a relationship that will last a lifetime.

Perhaps the best advice anyone ever gave is, "The next time you decide to develop a leader, begin your journey by becoming a friend."

22.

IF IT'S WEALTH YOU DESIRE
THE PLAN MUST COME FIRST

Money can't buy happiness. Money is the root of all evil. Money doesn't grow on trees. And on, and on, and still onward the "wacky wisdom" goes...

With all of this unconventional "enlightenment" floating around, is it any wonder that people are just a little confused when it comes to the subject of the almighty dollar?

Some time ago, I had the privilege of listening to David D'Arcangelo, a leading authority on money and wealth strategies. What surprised me about David's presentation wasn't his home-based business subject matter, or even his slant towards the rising popularity of Network Marketing—that's a given. What I found so intriguing, were his opening remarks about, well, money...

According to David, "The three most important

things we will ever learn in life are: 1) How to get a job; 2) How to communicate with the opposite sex; and, 3) How to handle our money."

And then he added this secondary sobering statement:

"For the most part, we learn each of these critical life lessons by trial and error."

> *"Apparently, it's not the money that you count first; it's the plan—because it's the plan that enables you to count the money."*

"Imagine," David boldly told his audience, "If doctors learned how to treat patients by trial and error—we would all be dead!" Now there's an interesting point to ponder!

What's going on here? Why are we as a society, so caught up with, and at the same time so downright confused by money, something we supposedly can't live with, and seemingly can't live without?

How about you? Do you have all this prosperity stuff figured out, or would we still find your financial house under construction?

Let's face it, our answers to this question can be a bit unpleasant.

Many years ago, before studying the subject, I believed the best solution to having more money was simply making more money. Today, having refined my thinking process, I now understand that "more" isn't usually what is needed... What is needed is a better plan for earning, and then holding on to a portion of all we create.

Jim Rohn, one of Tony Robbins' mentors, echoed the point: Student, "If I had more money, I would have a better plan." To which the teacher responded, "I would suggest that if you had a better plan, you would have more money."

Apparently, it's not the money that you count first; it's the plan—because it's the plan that enables you to count the money. *Interesting...*

So what about you? Do you have a plan?

My plan was discovered on a dusty old bookshelf, in an almost forgotten thrift store, a long, long time ago. Paid a quarter for it... A little booklet—containing the wisdom of Solomon—entitled, *Seven Cures for a Lean Purse*, by George S. Clason.

If the question inscribed on the cover, *If It's Wealth You Desire?* wasn't enough to grab my attention, certainly the words printed on the third page were:

"A message of vital importance to every man and woman with financial ambitions to accomplish and high ideals to uphold."

Didn't realize it at the time, but that masterpiece had already become a book by the same author, which to this day continues to be one of the best-selling written works of all time...

The Richest Man In Babylon.

Therefore, if it's wealth you desire... Acquire *The*

Richest Man In Babylon for your library. Read it. And then apply it in your life. The strategies are as timeless as they are brilliant, and now they're even printed on recycled paper.

23.

MAKE THIS YOUR BEST YEAR EVER
EIGHT SIMPLE STEPS TO
BUILDING A BETTER LIFE

The ball in Time Square has dropped, and brought to a close yet another year. Sadness for some—an ending, a conclusion, a finale. For others 'tis just the opposite... The beginning. A New Year. And indeed, one more chance to see if they can put it all together...

How about you? Were you able to kiss your true love as the clock struck twelve, or has life somehow left you wondering somewhere along the way? Wherever you find yourself, this can still become your best year ever. Even if you've broken a few New Year's resolutions in the past—even if you've broken them all!

On the next few pages you will find eight simple steps you can take to build a better life. And the good news is, that by investing about an hour per day—over the next 365 days—you can invent your own living masterpiece. After all, last year is history, and tomorrow without any planning will be a mystery... However, if you will go to work on the present, the future will be an incredible gift.

Design Your Year With The End In Mind

Your first order of business is to take out pen and paper. Next, go find your watch or some other timing device complete with second hand intact. And when I say "Go!" start writing everything you have ever wanted in life. For this exercise you're limited to just three minutes. Therefore, speed is your only concern. Try for 25 to 50 separate items like: the car you desire, that perfect home to call your own, perhaps some new friends, how much money you have in the bank, an amount of free time available to enjoy life, your contribution to society, church, or a foundation, the size of your organization, how many new business-builders will be joining you this year, etc. Now remember, keep this to exactly three minutes. Ready... Set... Go!

Welcome back... Now take a good look at your list, and by circling those items, choose the ten most important to you. Next, take out a clean sheet of paper, and rewrite each goal in present-tense language—as if it already were your reality. For example: "I drive a Chrysler Crossfire. My car is jet black with gray leather interior, and is equipped with every dealer option available." Keep in mind that every detail you leave out must be filled in by someone else, so unless you want to "drive a different car someday" be specific. Complete this exercise for each of the ten goals you've selected, and then move on to step two.

Set Aside 15 Minutes to Dream

We've all heard the sayings: "Crystallize your thinking." "We become what we think about." "Visualizing is realizing." And on it goes... Because nothing is stronger than a dream that pulls you right into the future. And what's the best way to add that absolute feeling to your dreams? You guessed it. Actual photographs, with you taking center stage.

Take your camera and go find your dream home, car, and life. Come up with your own way of uniquely placing yourself into the picture, and then have the photo lab print out some 8x10's. Plaster

> *"And the good news is, that by investing about an hour per day—over the next 365 days— you can invent your own living masterpiece."*

a wall in your home with this compelling vision of your future. And from that moment forward invest 15 minutes daily in front of your wall seeing every detail. Focus on what you desire. Discover, and then rediscover every dream, allowing them to entice you, mentally moving you forward with each passing day.

Read Ten Pages of a Great Book

Take your ten best goals, and decide which is the most important to you. Then go acquire a book that by its very title suggests it will draw you closer to the new vision of yourself. Consume ten to fifteen pages daily, until you have devoured and absorbed the author's knowledge. And immediately apply everything you possibly can, enjoying all the success this brings into your life.

Plan Your Work and Work Your Plan

The Quakers have a saying "When you pray, move your feet!" How true. Having a written plan, and even possessing the knowledge to carry it out, won't necessarily take you where you desire to go. You need to apply the "all out massive action" principle. You need to set up your calendar with the days and times you will plan your future, then read, dream, and *work* your business. Because sometimes it's easy to get faked out—always busy, busy, busy. But we must constantly be asking ourselves, "Busy doing what?"

Therefore, each night before you retire, decide in writing the six most important things you will do the following day. And in the morning ask yourself this question, "What is the most important task I can accomplish today?" With your answer in mind, go to work. When you have finished that assignment, move on to the next most important item, and so on, and so forth.

Spend Less Than You Earn; Invest The Difference

Pick up a copy of *The Richest Man in Babylon* and discover why "Money is plentiful for those who understand the simple rules of its acquisition." The seven principles revealed in this classic include: *Start thy purse to fattening. Control thy expenditures. Make thy gold multiply. Guard thy treasure from loss. Make of thy dwelling a profitable investment. Insure a future income. Increase thy ability to earn.* Because the simple truth is, it's not how much you earn, it's how much you keep. So if growing your financial portfolio is of interest to you, go get the book.

Invest Your Drive Time Wisely

As a society, we spend far too much time in our cars. And for most people that time is sadly wasted. In order to make this your best year ever, select your second most important goal and pick up a set of audiotapes or CDs on the subject. Commit to listening, applying, and growing as this new knowledge becomes a part of the very fabric of your mind. If you desire to earn more, you've got to learn more, and there is no better place to invest in your most valuable asset—you—than traveling up the road of life.

Always Move Towards Your Dream

With every decision you make this year, ask yourself two questions: "Will what I'm considering push me further from, or pull me closer towards my goals?" Only do those things that will draw you in the direction you've decided to go. And if your first answer is a resounding "closer towards," try asking this powerful follow-up question, "How would the person I desire to become, do the thing I'm about to do?" Deciding to act as the person you want to be will elevate your decisions to greatness.

Believe In Your Future

In 1948 Claude M. Bristol wrote an amazing book, *The Magic of Believing.* With a forward from then Editor and Publisher of The Denver Post, Palmer Hoyt, Bristol's work remains to this day as timeless as it is profound.

In the author's own words you will find this commanding revelation: "Just believe that there is genuine creative magic in believing—and magic there will be, for belief will supply the power which will enable you to succeed in everything you undertake. Back your belief with a resolute will and you become unconquerable." And yet it was Eleanor Roosevelt who may have said it best when she uttered these now immortal words, "The future belongs to those who believe in the beauty of their dreams." Indeed it does....

24.

THE 5% FORMULA
BECOME A SUCCESSFUL BUSINESS-BUILDER

M any years ago I had the pleasure of meeting, in my opinion, one of the very best success trainers in the world—a man by the name of Brian Tracy—in a seminar he was conducting here in Seattle.

During that event, Mr. Tracy asked his audience of several thousand somewhat successful attendees this philosophically profound question: "Why is it that some people are more successful than others?"

And, as expected, Mr. Tracy proceeded to explain the reasons people succeed, and don't succeed, in detail. He then provided the formula any of us could use in order to become a top 5% income earner in our chosen industry—in five years time—without a lot of effort on our part...

According to Mr. Tracy, all we needed to do was read 10 pages of good book every day, listen to 30 minutes of a great CD or audiotape every day and take at least one class per quarter—in the business-related field we desired to achieve success. Then if we simply applied what we learned, over the next five years we would find ourselves in the top 5% of the income earners in our chosen field.

Well, I took that advice, and I am able to report that Brian Tracy was right! And now it's your turn to achieve that same level of success by applying, *The 5% Formula.*

So if you're ready to build a world-class organization, and become a successful business-builder, here are the exact steps you too need to take:

> *"Successful business builders invest in themselves, and in their own personal growth and development."*

Read 10 pages of a good book every day: And if you're looking for a great place to start, visit nexera.com and select the "Your Library" link, or simply check out the resource pages in the back of this book.

Listen to 30 minutes of a great audio program every day: And if you're looking for a great place to start, visit nexera.com and select the "Success Store" link, or simply check out the resource pages in the back of this book.

Take a class at least four times every year: I'll be attending the next Mastermind event to learn everything I possibly can... (nexera.com/mastermind)

What about you?

You see, successful business-builders—and all those who want to become successful business-builders—simply select one area of their business to improve monthly, and then go to work on getting better! Because in our business, serious students of success are focused on mastering the fundamentals...

Prospecting: Do you have two new people to talk to every day?

Presentation: Are you enrolling your fair share?

Duplication: Are all those you're sponsoring doing the same?

Successful business-builders invest in themselves, and in their own personal growth and development, by applying *The 5% Formula.* Remember, successful business-builders select a book, listen to an audio program, or take a class so that the knowledge, insights, and wisdom they gain can transport them from wherever they currently are, to that future destination they ultimately desire to go... That's why we are willingly following them. That's why they are successful business-builders!

Therefore, if you're ready to become a successful business-builder too, take this advice: Select one area of your business or your life that you would like to improve, and then using the resources previously suggested, apply *The 5% Formula!*

Now let's go to work on your future....

ABOUT THE AUTHOR

Personally

Michael and his wife September were married in Salem, Oregon on May 6, 1978. They have two children: a son, Taylor, born in January, 1980 and a daughter, Ashley, born in December, 1981. Michael, September, Taylor, and Ashley moved to Seattle in 1986.

Professionally

Michael S. Clouse is the Editor-in-Chief of Nexera e-News™ and author of numerous books, audio programs and published articles on the subject of Network Marketing. An internationally recognized industry expert, Michael is a well respected business consultant, personal success coach, and dynamic educational speaker. His weekly online newsletter, Nexera e-News™ is read by tens of thousands of Network Marketing Professionals around the world.

THE FIFTH PRINCIPLE

"Is The Fifth Principle great stuff? Try this test: Buy 10. Give them to your people—even and especially your business prospects—and ask each of them to read it in 24 hours. (That's easy.) At the end of your current pay-period, subtract the costs of the books from the increase in your check. Use 10 percent of that amount to buy more books. Keep doing that for one year. Then do whatever you desire for the rest of your life."

—John Milton Fogg
Author of *The Greatest Networker in the World*

1 book $15
2 – 9 books $10 each
10 – 29 books $8 each
30 + books - please call

Shipping charges will be added to these prices.

To order yours: visit www.nexera.com/v
U.S.A. 1 888 639 3722 International +1 425 774 4264

YOUR 90 DAY GAME PLAN

Prospecting, presentation, duplication, leadership.

Listen to this step-by-step, connect-the-dots, build-your-business-faster audio program, and you'll learn:

1) how to get your business started right,
2) prospecting, presentation, and duplication, and
3) the secret to finding and developing leaders.

If you want to succeed in your business, listening to—and learning from—this audio training program is an absolute must!

To order yours: visit www.nexera.com/90
U.S.A. 1 888 639 3722 International +1 425 774 4264

Thinking Your Way To Success

"Change your thinking and you will change your life!"

This is the most powerful information on the mind I have ever assembled... It explains why only a few distributors succeed, *and* why far too many simply fail—and how you can use your mind to become one 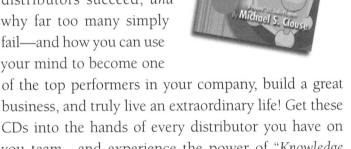 of the top performers in your company, build a great business, and truly live an extraordinary life! Get these CDs into the hands of every distributor you have on you team—and experience the power of *"Knowledge Applied!"*

This program contains three CDs, the complete PowerPoint outline, and includes, *"The 38 Philosophies"* bonus CD by Michael S. Clouse.

Your Prospecting Toolbox

"Learn where to find two new prospects every day—in any city you choose!"

To order yours: visit
www.nexera.com/ypt
U.S.A. 1 888 639 3722
International +1 425 774 4264

The Simple Art of Duplication

"What you need to know to build a business that duplicates!"

This program contains one CD, and features an interview with Art Jonak and Michael S. Clouse.

To order yours: visit www.nexera.com/art
U.S.A. 1 888 639 3722 International +1 425 774 4264

YOUR TOTAL SUCCESS PACK

Your Total Success Pack comes with seven of our best-selling audio programs, 19 CDs, the complete set of downloadable e-Books, and step-by-step instructions for each program!

These audio programs will teach you exactly how to create *Total Success* in your business and in your life! If you're ready to build a better future, order yours now!

Request Michael S. Clouse Live

If you coordinate your team's live training events and would like to request Michael S. Clouse as your guest speaker, simply e-mail the dates and details to info@nexera.com

Recipe For Success

Apply the simple, effective, and time-tested techniques revealed on this 75 minute training CD, and you will be able to easily go from the bottom 5% of the distributors in your company, to the top 5% of the distributors in your company, in less than five years!

To order yours: visit www.nexera.com/rfs
U.S.A. 1 888 639 3722 International +1 425 774 4264

AS A MAN THINKETH

Personal development authors
and teachers including: Jim
Rohn, Tony Robbins, Mark
Victor Hansen, Paul J. Meyer,
Earl Nightingale, Randy Gage,
and Denis Waitley, credit
this little book for providing
the foundation to their
principles...

As A Man Thinketh is, quite simply, a set of
philosophical reflections on the power of our thoughts...
According to James Allen, "All that a man acheives and
all that he fails to achieve is the direct result of his own
thoughts."

And now you can hear the story the way it was meant to
be told. Listen to the complete reading of this timeless
classic on CD, and receive the entire downloadable
e-Book as well. Order yours now!

FUTURE CHOICE
WHY NETWORK MARKETING
MAY BE YOUR BEST CAREER MOVE!

This book shows how Network Marketing fits today's hot trends of home-based businesses, entrepreneurship, and self-reliance. It paints a very compelling picture of the future of the business and the economic prosperity it can offer.

This is a great book to give to prospects, and it can also be used to build belief in new distributors.